Lasting Aalto Masterwork
The Library at Mount Angel Abbey

Donald Canty

6/16/92
To Rob from Papa Bear
All my love

Published by
Mount Angel Abbey
St. Benedict, Oregon

This Modest Tribute
is Dedicated to
Saint Benedict (480-548)
Founder of the Tradition
and
Howard Vollum (1913-1986)
and
Jean Vollum
Friends of the Tradition

International Standard Book Number 0-918941-04-0
Library of Congress Catalog Number 92-080534
©MCMXCII by Mount Angel Abbey
St. Benedict, Oregon, 97373
Produced by: Graphic Arts Center Publishing Company and Lincoln & Allen
Book Productions
President: Charles M. Hopkins
Editor-in-chief: Douglas A. Pfeiffer
Managing Editor: Jean Andrews
Project Director: Richard L. Owsiany
Designer: Leslie E. Holcomb
Separations: Wy'east Color, Inc.
Printer: Bridgetown Printing Co.
Bindery: Lincoln & Allen
Printed in the United States of America

Distributed to the trade
by Graphic Arts Center Publishing Company
P.O. Box 10306, Portland, Oregon, 97210
503/226-2402

The black and white photographs of the library were taken shortly after its completion by Morley Baer of Carmel, California.
The color photographs of the library were taken for this publication by Strode/Eckert Photographic of Portland, Oregon.
Photographs of other Aalto work on Pages 17 and 18 are by Phillip Jacobson, FAIA.
Drawings on Page 26 are by Timothy B. McDonald.

Donald Canty is architecture critic of the Seattle *Post-Intelligencer* and Pacific Northwest correspondent of *Progressive Architecture* magazine. He was for 15 years editor-in-chief of *Architecture*, magazine of the American Institute of Architects, and before that was editor-in-chief of *City* magazine, managing editor of *Architectural Forum,* and editor-in-chief of *Western Architect and Engineer.* He has been author and/or editor of four books on architecture and urban affairs, the most recent, *American Architecture in the 1980s*, published by the AIA Press.

A singular building sits astride the rim of a wooded butte in the beautiful Willamette Valley of Oregon, some forty miles south of Portland. It is the library of Mount Angel Abbey, a Benedictine monastery, and it was designed by Alvar Aalto of Finland, one of the early giants of modern architecture.

The abbey stands upon the top of the butte, a small assemblage of pleasant but architecturally undistinguished brick buildings arranged around a large central lawn, with a solidly massed chapel as the centerpiece.

The library, despite its distinguished architectural lineage, does not announce itself with any drama. If anything it is deferential to the rest of the little complex of buildings. On the north edge of the lawn, it is a single-story building of similar but lighter brick than the rest, meticulously proportioned but simple and rectilinear in form. Windows are covered with redwood grills, and the glazed entry is accentuated by a broad metal portico, trellised at each end. The building has a feeling of great repose.

On the opposite side, where the hill falls away, the façade is more dynamic. Here the building thrusts forward in four segments on three levels over a recessed basement. There are three bands of windows, one open and two screened.

Entry is through a plainspoken foyer with offices on one side and an auditorium on the other. Directly ahead, the drama begins. Past a

– Continued on page 12 –

The fan-shaped library is on the north edge of the hilltop abbey, in the foreground of the photo at left and the background of the photo above. On the following pages, the library's sharp profile, the view from below and its hilltop façade.

sculptural control desk, the building explodes into a three-story volume as it drops down the hillside site, taking the shape of a fan at the rear.

Book stacks radiate into the central well of space like spokes of a wheel. Continuous reading benches arc around the edge of the well at the main level and a partial mezzanine below.

Walls are rough, board-formed concrete, painted white; ceilings, smooth white plaster. Railings are dark metal, and there is an abundance of light wood trim. Everywhere there is soft natural light.

Beneath the ceiling at the rear of the main level is a continuous band of glass, admitting views of the sky and the surrounding trees, its light reflecting from the canted ceiling onto open carrels below. On the lower level, light enters from closed carrels with slat-screened windows and thence through translucent panels, giving the effect of a double wall.

On the main level, three small windows in the interstices of the fan's four segments frame views of fields and distant mountains like miniature paintings. And overhead is a semicircular skylight facing north, its light also reflecting softly off the ceiling into the space.

Three pairs of round columns rise amid the stacks. Three single columns rise through the mezzanine to meet exposed segments of the radial structure overhead, forming towering objects that again are like pieces of sculpture.

– Continued on page 16 –

Looking upward from one of the handsome, slanting stairways leading to the lower level there is a dramatic succession of arcs: the mezzanine, the edge of the main level, a wood-slat screen over the desk, the ceiling with its slashing skylight.

The heart of the library is this central multilevel space, seemingly always in motion and yet somehow restful and lavishly luminescent. Descending into it is descending into a world apart, a world of books, which is exactly what Aalto had in mind.

The following pages tell of the library in more detail and in the context of Aalto's work and modern architecture in general. They also tell of the abbey and how it came to seek and secure the services of the world-famed architect. They tell of the evolution of the design and the highly unusual way in which the design was realized over thousands of miles separating the architects from the client and the site. Finally, they tell of the remarkable impact that the library has had over its generation of use.

Throughout Alvar Aalto's illustrious career, chroniclers and theorists of architecture didn't quite know what to make of him. He was clearly responsive to nature and to his nation's rich vernacular architecture, and early showed a bent toward classicism. When the modern movement came along, with its calls for rationalism and functionalism, he responded with enthusiasm and became one of its acknowledged leaders.

He subscribed to modernism's theories, but he could seldom quite stay within the rigidly rectilinear, unadorned boundaries of its aesthetics. The romantic in him burst out in irregular, often curving, forms and decorative details. He was a bear of a man and a giant of a talent, and he went his own way. He was also a dedicated humanist. "True architecture, the real thing, exists only where man stands at the center," he said.

The knowledgeable author and editor, Stanley Abercrombie, has written that "Aalto was more than a master of artistic form and intelligent planning; he was the master as well of the details that relate a building successfully to its users. He cared for the proper shape of a handrail, for the convenience of storage elements, for the texture of a wall, and for the delights of natural light. . . . In Aalto's work we find an honorable and simple humanism among modernism's pretensions."

Even before World War II, Aalto had written that "most modern buildings neither fulfill their social function satisfactorily nor speak a language their users can understand." In the 1950s, he railed against "modern formalism where inhuman elements are dominating."

Such sentiments did not endear him to the modernists, whose glass and metal buildings were dominating the architectural press at the time. Later they struck a responsive chord in the postmodernists, whose prophet, Robert Venturi, praised Aalto for his "sensitivity to natural materials, fine detailing and willful picturesqueness."

Yet Aalto cannot be appropriated posthumously into the ranks of the post-modernists. His work was too disciplined, too rooted in social and functional concerns, for that.

It defies easy categorization. He was contemporary architecture's ultimate indi-vidualist. He didn't do modern buildings; he didn't do postmodern buildings. He did Aalto buildings.

When the monks of Mount Angel contacted him in the early 1960s, Aalto was at the height of his fame, perhaps the best-known Finn besides Sibelius, and a national hero in a nation that valued design. His mail regularly contained requests for him to take on commissions around the world, most of which he declined. His office was overburdened, and his doctor had counseled him to get more rest. Why should he agree to do a library in a remote part of America for a monastery whose population did not far exceed one hundred at a given moment?

One reason clearly was that Aalto loved to design libraries. They were among his favorite building types, a fact which his friend and principal biographer, Göran Schildt, links to his lifelong love of literature. Reading aloud was a custom in his home when he was growing up, and he continued it with his own children.

Above—Natural light bounces off reflective surfaces at Aalto's great Finnish Technical Institute at Otaniemi.

Above—The conical skylights were used at Otaniemi and in other Aalto libraries preceding Mount Angel.

His goal in library design was to create environments which supported "interaction with books," according to Schildt. The users needed "to easily find the right book and be able to read it in satisfactory lighting."

He had developed a very particular approach to achieving these goals, first devised for a 1927 competition for a library in Viipuri. He refined this approach over the years and used it in Mount Angel's immediate predecessor libraries in Seinajoki and Rovaniemi.

One element of this approach was use of reflected natural light to avoid glare, bringing it in more from the ceiling than through conventional windows in the walls. For the Viipuri library he invented a cone-shaped skylight in which light first played against the walls of the cone and then downward. He used it in all of the succeeding libraries.

Another element was placement of reading areas in multilevel wells or "pits" surrounded by books. Aalto's earlier libraries were on flat sites, and the changing levels of the reading areas had to be built from the ground up.

But at Mount Angel the hillside site and the need for most of the building to hang over its edge virtually mandated a deep central reading area. It must have been a library site that Aalto found hard to resist. He also could be expected to respond to the Benedictine monks' attitude toward the significance of libraries and books.

Monasteries have been the conservators of culture and learning throughout Christian history. The order of monks founded by Saint Benedict in the sixth century "has a particular devotion to libraries and book-oriented culture," wrote Lawrence McCrank in his 1983 history of Mount Angel Abbey. It has been a history marked by both tragedy and tenacity.

The Mount Angel Abbey was founded in 1882 by monks from the seven-hundred-year-old Benedictine monastery in Engelberg, Switzerland. Some Swiss monasteries had been suppressed, and the monks felt the need for a potential refuge in the new world.

They saw in the three-hundred-foot butte in Fillmore, a small rural town with a substantial Swiss and German population, later renamed Mount Angel, a nearly perfect monastery site. They built a gabled priory and church at the base of the site. They built of wood, and in 1892 the buildings were all but destroyed by fire, a near-fatal blow to the new monastery.

The monks persevered and began to build anew, this time at the top of the hill. They also rebuilt the contents of their library into a collection of some twenty thousand volumes. Then a second fire struck in 1926, and the process of rebuilding had to begin again. One by one, the present buildings rose, built more solidly, and somewhat more stolidly, than before.

For more than forty years, however, they did not include a library. The monastery's book collection, ravaged by the second fire but again painstakingly restored, was scattered throughout the monastery and its college and seminary.

The abbey did, however, acquire its first professionally trained librarian in the person of an imaginative monk named Barnabas Reasoner. Upon taking the post in 1953, he began a sustained campaign for a new library building. He found a receptive ear in then-Abbot Damian Jentges who "saw the library as a key to establishing the abbey as a cultural and educational force," according to a thesis on the library building by Reed College student Jonathan Felix Gelber. In 1962 the abbot authorized the librarian to proceed with planning and fund-raising for a new library that would "make the hilltop a regional cultural center and recapture some of the monastery's older aspirations."

The preliminary program for the library began by saying that "in keeping with the Benedictine monastic tradition it is to be a focal point of Mount Angel Abbey second only to the church." It was to serve the 104 students of the abbey's liberal arts college, 41 students in its postgraduate theology program, and 120 monks, plus lay faculty members and visitors.

There was to be room for expansion. The collection at the time comprised fifty thousand bound volumes; expansion to two hundred thousand was envisioned. But in the meantime, the program stated, "We do not wish to sacrifice the atmosphere of friendly privacy for rows of empty stacks or barren areas."

"We are traditionally lovers of books and learning," the program continued, and "the architect should be allowed complete freedom to create a building worthy of our monastic tradition and of the natural beauty of the setting of Mount Angel." The building "should have a unique and distinctive note in keeping with its use by a twentieth-century Benedictine community."

Father Barnabas, it turned out, had architectural aspirations not previously evidenced on the hilltop. If Mount Angel were going to have a new library, why shouldn't it have the best? And this, of course, meant getting the best available architect.

The best available *contemporary* architect, he emphasized. Winds of change were sweeping the church and were to culminate in the Second Vatican Council with its call for the Catholic faithful to "live in very close union with the men of their time" and "strive to understand perfectly their way of thinking and feeling as expressed in their culture." In particular, "efforts must be made so that those who practice the arts can feel that the church gives recognition to them and their activities."

Father Barnabas was not particularly *au courant* with contemporary architecture, his architectural interests having arisen through an interest in history. So he set about to search for

the right person, reading architectural journals and talking to those more in touch. The names of Louis Kahn and I. M. Pei came up, and so did that of Alvar Aalto.

Aalto was a legend in his native land and among the architectural cognoscenti worldwide, but his name was hardly a household word in America. He had done only one building in the United States, a respected postwar dormitory at M.I.T. His name was, however, well known among librarians. Father Barnabas had come across a photograph of the Viipuri library in a librarians' journal and had been impressed by Aalto's "intelligent regard for books and reading. This was a real library, not just another building." He was also impressed with Aalto's handling of natural light, an important consideration in Oregon's often gray climate. In 1963 Aalto was awarded the gold medal, highest honor of the American Institute of Architects. This sealed Father Barnabas's choice and also gave him hope that the honor might incline Aalto to look favorably on the idea of undertaking another project in the United States.

And so he wrote to Aalto in terms that could hardly have been better crafted to attract the humanistic and nature-loving Finn. He reminded Aalto of the Benedictine tradition of excellence, then said: "We need you. We have this magnificent monastic site and we don't want to spoil it. We want you to improve our site and give us a building that will fulfill our needs in a beautiful and intelligent way."

A postal strike in Finland delayed receipt of the letter and Aalto's response. Some of the monks were skeptical that the great architect would take the commission and concerned that he might ask a large fee. Some found unseemly "worldliness" in turning to such a famous designer.

Finally Aalto responded: "I am very interested in your suggestion as libraries are my favorite subject." He said that he could not come to America but that he had a young Finnish associate, Eric Vartiainen, who had been educated at the University of California and who could come and act as his liaison. He suggested Vernon DeMars of Berkeley, who had been Vartiainen's teacher and a close friend of Aalto's during a teaching stint at M.I.T., as architect of record, since if the library were officially a project of Aalto's firm he would have had to come to Oregon to take a licensing examination like any recent architectural school graduate.

The DeMars firm would handle the engineering of the building and preparation of construction documents and share supervision of the building process with Vartiainen. All concerned understood, however, that in the words of DeMars, "this was not to be an 'Aalto-inspired design' by an American firm but as genuinely an Aalto building as though it had been completely carried out by his own office in Helsinki."

The monks sent Aalto the program, photographs, contour maps of the site, and other materials, and the process of design began in Helsinki. The first version was delivered to the monastery in May 1964. It was somewhat at variance with the program, so Vartiainen, then working on an Aalto office interiors project at the Institute of International Education in New York, was sent to meet with the monks and make any necessary revisions, taking the new drawings back to Helsinki for approval.

Vartiainen subsequently moved into the DeMars office, bringing with him a bulging file of detail drawings from previous Aalto libraries. As the design evolved in Helsinki, drawings were sent to Berkeley, where details were worked out in accordance with American engineering and building practices. Sometimes design changes were proposed from Berkeley but always for Aalto's personal approval. Vartiainen would go periodically to Mount Angel to meet with the monks and gather information and reactions, then return to Helsinki to work with Aalto on the design.

All of this took time, and the monks were growing restive. In 1966 Father Barnabas wrote in his "library bulletin" that "the endless delay and the postponement of the project over the last three years has caused us to lose a little of our good humor and enthusiasm." He visited DeMars in Berkeley, who suggested that Aalto, "a warm and gregarious personality," responded best to personal

– Continued on page 26 –

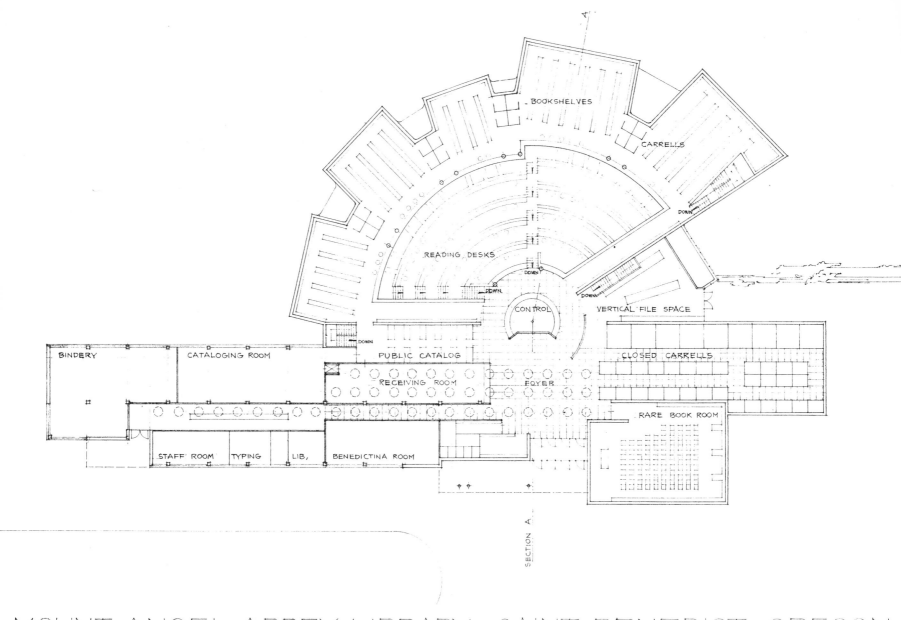

MOUNT ANGEL ABBEY LIBRARY, SAINT BENEDICT, OREGON,
GROUND - FLOOR   16 FT/ = 1 INCH   HELSINKI 9, 5, 1964 ALVAR AALTO, ARCHITECT,

Above—In this early design for the library, of which there were four before the final version was developed, there are five reading levels and a tower-like skylight over the main control desk. The fan shape and central well of space were part of the design from the beginning but use and configuration of spaces changed.

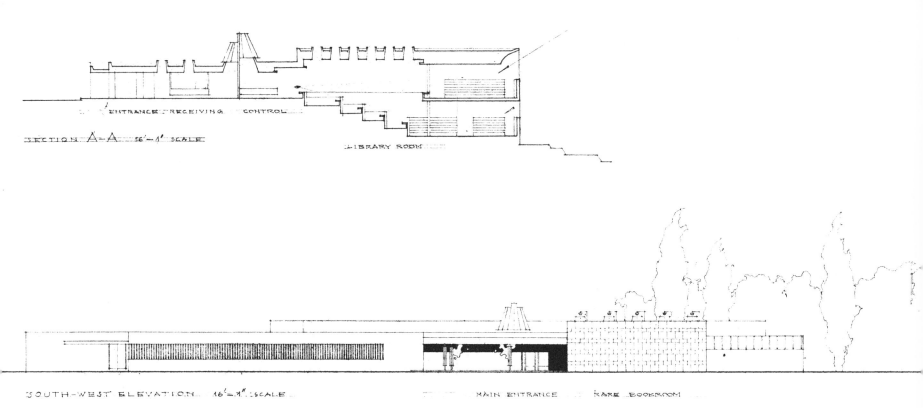

ENTRANCE RECEIVING CONTROL

SECTION A-A 16'=1" SCALE

LIBRARY ROOM

SOUTH-WEST ELEVATION 16'=1" SCALE

MAIN ENTRANCE RARE BOOKROOM

MOUNT ANGEL ABBEY LIBRARY, SAINT BENEDICT, OREGON,

HELSINKI 9/5/1964 ALVAR AALTO, ARCHITECT,

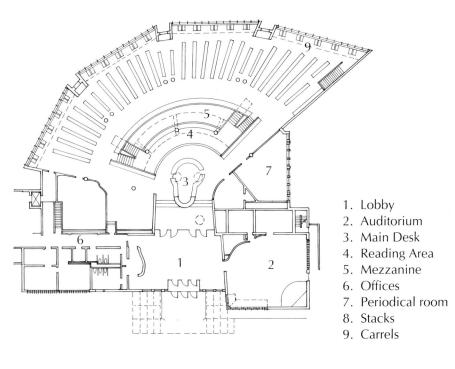

1. Lobby
2. Auditorium
3. Main Desk
4. Reading Area
5. Mezzanine
6. Offices
7. Periodical room
8. Stacks
9. Carrels

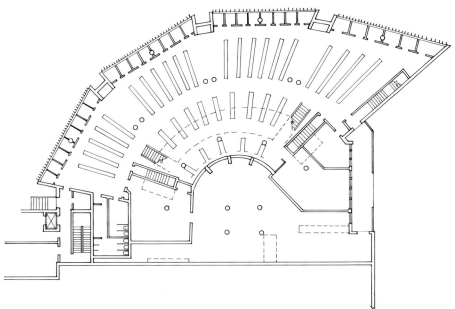

The final plan, upper level top, lower level above.

contact. Abbot Damian agreed that Father Barnabas should go to Helsinki "to expedite the project." An unspoken purpose of the trip was to reassure Aalto that the library actually would be built. The monastery had less than a third of the project's estimated cost.

Father Barnabas found Aalto in Zurich looking "terribly tired" and, at 69, in failing health. Yet he was able to report on his return that "there is no doubt whatsoever that Aalto is most interested in his Oregon project." Aalto promised to visit the site as soon as his doctor permitted. The design was nearing completion.

The library had taken its basic shape from the start but the arrangement of spaces inside had gone through five changes. In the early version shown on previous pages there were five levels to the reading well—it looked like an inverted Greek theater, a form that had always interested Aalto. The ceiling over the well was an almost unbroken array of the cone skylights and a taller parabolic skylight above the main desk rose as a tower, increasing the library's presence on the hilltop. Carrels were in the space where the auditorium is now and in the largest segment of the fan, of which there were then five of irregular depth.

Budget problems caused the size of the building to be reduced and the fan foreshortened. In the process of revision, the design moved toward its final form. The fan

– Continued on page 28 –

was simplified and further splayed, its segments reduced to four of even depth. The levels of the well were reduced to two plus a mezzanine, and the semicircular skylight was introduced above it. The carrels took their place on the periphery.

There remained the matter of money. In 1967 Father Barnabas asked the abbot for permission to seek it from Howard and Jean Vollum, friends of the abbey and co–founders of the leading Portland area firm, Tektronix. The abbot gave his approval but warned Father Barnabas that he had previously approached the Vollums for building funds and had been turned down. This time, however, Father Barnabas had an Aalto building to propose, and the Vollums donated one million dollars in stock for its construction and later gave additional funds for its operation.

Left—Alvar Aalto on what was to be his only visit to the abbey. Below—Aalto and architect of record Vernon DeMars speaking to local architects and students.

Also in 1967 Aalto came to the United States to receive still another honor, the Thomas Jefferson architectural medal. He took the occasion to make his first and only visit to Mount Angel. On arrival he stood silently on the library site for a long time. Finally he said: "It's like an acropolis, more beautiful than I imagined." He noticed that a fine stand of evergreens on the east side of the site was marked for removal. "We must save those trees," he said. An aide asked, "But how? They are directly in the way." Aalto replied,

"Move the building," and the site was shifted ten feet to the west.

During his two-day visit, the decidedly non-verbal Aalto reluctantly agreed to address a gathering of local architects and architectural students. He spoke of his feeling for libraries, saying that they last while other types of buildings fade away. "The church is number one, then comes the library." Of his use of daylight he said, "I try to get light which spreads in the room so that no matter at which angle you hold the book there will never be hard reflection in your eyes." Someone mentioned the similarity of the Mount Angel library to its predecessors in Finland, and he said that he did not mind using good ideas more than once. Asked why the library did not have larger glass areas to make the most of the magnificent views, he replied, "I have designed a place of study, not a lounge."

Some of the monks had similar reservations about this aspect of the design, feeling that views to the north were being taken from them and not admitted to the library. Early on, Father Barnabas had written of "a picture window" looking out to the views. But behind Aalto's ready reply to his questioner was a deep conviction that library design, especially in an academic setting, should remove all possible distractions from serious work.

He put a large window in the periodical room, which is as much lounge as workplace, and he put the three small view windows in

Right—Aalto and one of the trees that he moved the building to save. Below—Aalto with Father Barnabas at the abbey.

niches between segments of the fan. But that was as far as he would go.

There were also some questions among the monks about the multilevel design requiring much walking up and down stairs with sometimes heavy loads of books (there is only a single service elevator). And some wondered why the more dramatic, angular, north façade was placed where few would see it except at a distance. But when the monks voted on the final design, it was easily approved.

Structural design was in the hands of San Francisco engineer Stephen Medwedowski. His scheme, readily adopted by Aalto, called for the pairs of columns supporting radiating beams, with the upper level cantilevered over the well, and single columns supporting the semicircular skylight. Some modernists might have exposed the beams in the name of structural "honesty," but Aalto felt that they would have been redundant to the radiating stacks.

The project was not put out to bid. The firm of Reimers and Jolivette of Portland was chosen as contractor, largely because of its work on the churches of the famed Northwest architect Pietro Belluschi. When construction began, Vartiainen moved into guest quarters at the monastery to supervise the work on a day-to-day basis and make whatever design modifications were necessary. DeMars, his partner John Wells, and Medwedowski also visited the site regularly.

The workmen sensed that they were creating a building of significance, and the level of craftsmanship throughout was high. The building was completed in 1970 at a cost of $1,272,000, a modest $32,000 over budget. Aalto's fee was $18,000, also a modest figure. At the dedication there was a blessing by the archbishop of Portland and addresses by the head of the Benedictine order and the Finnish ambassador to America, a lecture by an Oxford historian, and concerts by a college choir, a youth symphony—and the Duke Ellington Orchestra. Ellington was persuaded to come by a friend and local composer, Ann Henry, and gave the premier performance of one of her works.

Aalto could not attend the dedication. He died in 1976 without ever seeing the library. However, his wife, Elissa, also an architect and a close collaborator on many Aalto projects, saw the library in 1980 on the occasion of a major exhibition of his work held at Mount Angel. She later wrote, "When I stood in the library hall and felt the combined effect of space and light, I knew that we had designed a good building." Critics agreed. *Architectural Record* magazine wrote of "the complete individuality of the solution based on the uniqueness of the building's requirements and of its site." The Belgian Dom Frederick Debuyst called the library "an absolute, radical refusal of mediocrity." Ada Louise Huxtable, then America's leading architectural critic, wrote in the New York Times that the library was "a small and perfect work." She said that it represented "a kind of architecture that is elegant, humane and full of sophisticated skills . . . Vintage Aalto—subtle, sensuous, full of wisdom about the environment and man."

The library is held in great esteem by the monks. A catalogue for the seminary said that "we are fortunate to be heirs to a very long and great tradition of Benedictine libraries. From this we gain certain convictions about what a library should be. First of all, we believe that a library must be a place of peace and a place that gives visual delight . . . a source of liberty and refreshment. Our library is a space which makes one want to sit and read."

The building has changed remarkably little over the years. It remains rich in details and experiences. The distinctive Aalto detailing begins at the entrance portico where steel columns are wrapped in wood strips. The hefty brass door handles, which fit the hand firmly and comfortably were designed by Aalto and fabricated for the library. The floor of the lobby, which doubles as an exhibit space, is dark brick and its walls white-painted brick in contrast to the light tan brick outside. The walls slant inward slightly, subtly guiding the eye toward the drama of the great central space. Coatroom and restroom doors are shielded from view by a sinuously curving, slatted-wood screen. In Finnish, *aalto* means "wave."

– Continued on page 36 –

Above—A characteristic Aalto detail, metal columns on the portico clad in wood.

Above—The hefty Aalto-designed brass handles on the entry doors.

Above—Meticulously crafted wood slat screen conceals a firehose.

Above—The enclosed, light-filled carrels on the lower floor.

Above—The open carrels on the perimeter of the upper floor.

Above—The main desk with its deep conical skylights and wood screen overhead.

This space and the work areas to the left are illuminated by cone skylights, and there is also track lighting in the lobby for exhibits. To the right is the hundred-seat auditorium/lecture hall, a warm, enveloping space whose every element bespeaks Aalto. A fan-shaped screen of slats with curved edges hangs from the ceiling, stopping just short of the side walls and at the outer edge of the seating. The edges of the screen trace another wave. Behind the small stage, another screen sweeps sharply upward. This one is solid and in the shape of a longer, narrower fan. Walls alternate concrete and burlap. Windows are at opposite corners of the room, high against the ceiling, which is again canted to reflect light inward. The Aalto-designed light fixtures have brass reflectors.

The lobby ends at the finely crafted control desk which takes roughly the shape of a pear. It is a handsome, undulating object, and it gives librarians views of all three levels of the main space. The screen over the desk, also of wood slats with curved edges, is penetrated by more of the cone skylights. From here the central well reads as a single, unified space, reaching out to the edges of the fan, given added dynamism by the intervention of the mezzanine. At reading counters on the main floor and mezzanine are individual, Aalto-designed reading lamps. There are fluorescent lights in the upper edges of the stacks and recessed ceiling lights. Hidden fluorescents

– *Continued on page 42* –

Above—The auditorium's curving wood wall. Overleaf, the auditorium in use.

Above—The periodical room with its fine collection of Aalto furniture has the library's largest window.

Above—One of the small view windows between segments of the fan.

above the mezzanine shine upward against the same reflective surfaces that diffuse daylight. There are also exterior light fixtures above the cone skylights so that they glow by night at least as interestingly as by day.

Fine details abound. Here a metal rail wraps around a column; there a slatted screen shields a fire hose cabinet. Corners likely to be touched by human hands are edged in wood. The closed carrels on the lower level are tiny but wonderfully luminous spaces, in constant demand. The indentations between the fan's segments give the areas between stacks and exterior walls on the upper level, where the open carrels are located, the feeling of rooms. The finishing touch is that the ends of the stacks, which can be utilitarian and unattractive and which are very visible here, are covered with handsome wood-slat screens, which in places extend above stacks for emphasis.

Color is left to the books; the library's palette is white, black, and gray. But any hint of austerity is removed by the warmth of natural woods: fir, birch, hemlock, and oak, with a touch of redwood outside. And everywhere are examples of Aalto's skill as a furniture designer: this is America's largest single collection of Aalto furniture, which is nearly as highly regarded as his architecture.

The library has had significant impact on the monastery. It has attracted a steady flow of grants and bequests; the collection has grown greatly. There is a steady outflow of interlibrary loans, a constant stream of visitors, some at the abbey for retreats or for the annual Bach festival started after the library's construction.

But the impact goes deeper than the quantifiable. At a meeting of monks who had been at the abbey during the library's design and construction, convened for purposes of this publication, one said: "It set a new standard of excellence for everything that we do." Another said, "People have expected more of us since the library was built. It drives us to respond at a higher level than before. It has created an upward cycle of expectations and response."

A monk who was a seminary student at Mount Angel when the library was built credits it with drawing him into the Benedictine order and the abbey. "I am grateful to the building," he says. "It is a symbol of the aspirations of the abbey. It challenges us to achieve a higher level of endeavor." Another said, "I've used it almost every day for twenty years, and it lifts my spirits every time."

The library, in all, is quintessential Aalto: in the furniture and details; in the virtuoso play of light; in the curving forms and swirling spaces; in the tension between the disciplined, rationalist south façade and the angular, romantic north, jutting out from the hillside like a craggy boulder; above all in its friendliness to users. If one had to pick a single building to elucidate Aalto's design approach, it might well be the Mount Angel Abbey library.